THE LOCH NESS MONSTER

Loch Ness is one of the most famous tourist sites in the world – not simply because of its stunning beauty, but mostly because of the mystery of the 'Monster' that may lurk in its waters. Known affectionately as 'Nessie', this elusive creature has been chased with great zeal for most of the 20th century, and this enthusiasm shows no sign of diminishing.

A monster at Loch Ness was first chronicled in AD 565, in an episode concerning the Irish missionary-saint Columba. According to his biographer, St Adamnan (who wrote a century afterwards), one of St Columba's disciples was swimming across the River Ness to fetch a boat for his master. Suddenly, a monster broke the surface, 'with a great roar and open mouth'. Not unnaturally, the onlookers were 'stricken with great terror', but St Columba made the sign of the cross, saying: 'Think not to go further, nor touch thou that man. Quick, go back...'

The creature obeyed. The saint's intervention seems to have been extraordinarily effective, for in the 1400 intervening years, the Monster has not only refrained from attacking any of its dozens of witnesses, but has been remarkably silent, too. It roars no more.

by Lynn Picknett

Out of the Depths

No fewer than 265 of the world's lakes and rivers have been reported to harbour similar 'monsters'; sites as far apart as Canada and the Congo boast their own shy beasts, and within the British Isles Cornish and Irish monsters continue to be reported, not to mention strange creatures of the surrounding seas. But of all the world's 'monster' sites, no fewer than 24 are to be found in Scotland alone.

Perhaps it is because there is something inherently mysterious about the land of dramatically shifting sunlight and swirling mists. Or there may be a more mundane explanation for the attractiveness of its countryside to strange beasts: certainly the unique geology of Loch Ness provides scope for even the most elusive to live undetected.

The loch lies at the northern end of the Great Glen fault line that cuts across the Highlands of Scotland. It is the greatest volume of fresh water in the UK; 52 feet (16m) above sea level, 24 miles long and one mile wide, it is connected to the sea by the River Ness.

Loch Ness is intensely cold – never a comfortable place to swim except for the hardiest or most masochistic – very deep, and so clotted with peat that visibility extends only a few feet. Until the late 1960s the deepest part of the loch was believed to be 754 feet (230m), but an underwater investigation by the Vickers *Pisces* submersible (1969) claimed to have reached a depth of 820 feet (250m) and had recorded a further depth by sonar of 975 feet (297m). And Project Ercot have claimed a depth of 846 feet (258m) but this is yet to be confirmed.

The top 100 feet (30m) can heat up to around 12°C (54°F) in summer, but below that the depths never vary in temperature beyond more than half a degree, remaining at around 5.5°C (42°F). Not surprisingly, most aquatic life – fish, seals and so on – is to be found close to the surface, and until the 1980s, the bottom of the loch was believed to be totally devoid of any sort of creature. However, in 1981 the Loch Ness Project discovered a population of Arctic charr living at a depth in excess of 700 feet (214m). And if the peaty depths hold such unexpected secrets, what else may they be hiding?

BELOW: *Sonar detection has discovered a population of Arctic Charr which have lived undetected since the melting of the ice more than 12,000 years ago.*

LEFT: *The sonar boat of scientist Adrian Shine. Years of research have shown that underwater 'contacts' of huge dimensions may be caused by side echoes from the steep walls of the loch.*

BELOW: *Loch Ness depth chart (metres).*

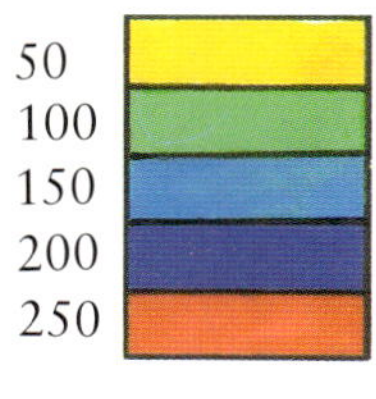

To many, the notion of a monster lurking in a British lake is utterly ridiculous. We can put men on the Moon, transplant organs from one person to another and talk to our friends on another continent – so how can there possibly be some kind of unknown monster within 540 miles of London?

Such sceptics, of course, dismiss all historical descriptions of similar beasts as ignorant superstition. But it was less than 200 years ago that French scientists were equally dismissive of peasants' descriptions of great stones falling from the sky onto the countryside. The scientists refused to do so much as to get out of their armchairs to investigate – because how could stones fall from the sky when there are no stones in the sky? Yet even without the permission of such great men, meteorites continued to fall.

Perhaps the despised historical records do, after all, hold clues as to the true nature of 'Nessie'.

Descriptions of the Monster have, for the most part, been consistent. It is said to

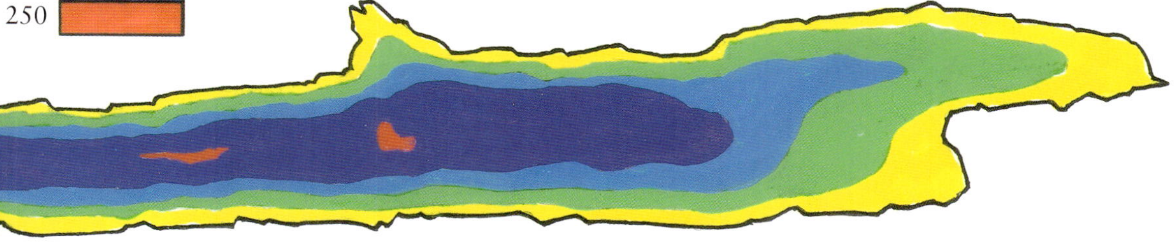

RIGHT: *In 1933 reported sightings of the Monster caused such interest that this cage was constructed to capture it.*

Dragons and Worms

have a bulky, dark body, and a long, serpentine neck. Its head has been described as 'small and sheep-like', and when it moves through the water its back is sometimes seen as two or more distinct humps. All of this seems remarkably similar to ancient descriptions of 'dragons' and 'worms', which once – legend has it – infested the British countryside.

Traditionally, these beasts guarded treasure at the bottom of the sea or in underground caverns. They were loathsome and fearsome, and came to represent the powers of darkness, to be overcome by the power of light – Christianity. To kill a dragon was, therefore, not only an heroic achievement, but a triumph of good over evil itself. Legends record how most of the great heroes – Sigurd, Beowulf, Siegfried, King Arthur, Tristan, St George and St Michael – all slew dragons, to their greater glory and that of God.

Most dragons were huge and horrible. One, at Lyminster in Sussex, was trapped by a poisoned pudding that was so large it had to be carried on a cart. The greedy monster snapped up the lot – including the horse and cart.

One of the most famous British legends of dragons is that of the 'Lambton Worm' ('worm' is an Old English alternative to 'dragon') of County Durham. Back in the mists of time, the Lambton heir went fishing on a Sunday. His catch proved disappointing – just a strange, eel-like creature – and he threw it down a well. Time passed, and young Lambton went off on a Crusade, blissfully unaware that the 'eel' had grown to a monstrous size, broken out of the well, and was happily devouring the youth of the county. On his return, Lambton met a witch, who promised to let him slay the dragon, but only on condition that he also killed the first creature he set eyes on after the heroic deed was done. The 'worm' duly despatched, Lambton turned to see his father, whom he had to kill according to his vow. But he reneged on his deal with the witch, resulting in a family curse which is said to be still in force.

Many mythical beasts still allegedly roam the world, pursued by fascinated, and ever hopeful, 'crypto-zoologists'. These

creatures include the famous Yeti and Bigfoot, besides the lesser-known Swamp Ape, Skunk Ape and Momo the Missouri Monster.

The Yeti or 'Abominable Snowman' is said to be a tall, hairy cross between an ape and a man that inhabits the foothills of the Himalayas. Like Nessie and many other such elusive monsters, the Yeti has long featured in the legend and myth of the indigenous people - in this case, the Sherpas. But since the 1950s, Western climbers have added to the excitement by witnessing unknown ape-like beasts scurrying over the rocks with extraordinary speed and agility, and have provided photographs of their tracks. As usual, however, sceptics have pounced, dismissing such evidence as misidentification of known species, hallucination or hoax.

Similarly, although the north American Bigfoot (and others of its ilk) have long been accepted by the Indians, much of the modern evidence – which includes a short film of a Bigfoot running away – is too inconclusive to cheer monster hunters. It seems that such creatures are almost abnormally shy or that there is a jinx on those who collect evidence for their existence.

BELOW: *In 1955 the famous 'three-humped' sighting was made close to the ruins of Urquhart Castle.*

No Shadow of Doubt

Generation after generation of the world's seamen have reported terrifying encounters with sea monsters, some so large as to engulf a wooden ship. One such was the legendary kraken, said to enjoy itself by plucking sailors off the deck of their ship one by one before swallowing the vessel whole. However, even the keenest of modern cryptozoologists might be forgiven for not taking too seriously old Norwegian claims that the kraken was a mile long, and its undulations often mistaken for floating islands!

Nearer home, at least metaphorically, is the sea-serpent. In the 4th century BC Aristotle wrote: 'Mariners sailing along the coast have told how they have seen the bones of many oxen which ... had been devoured by serpents. And as their ships sailed on, the serpents came to attack them, some of them throwing themselves on a trireme [a ship with three rows of oars on either side] and capsizing it.'

Over the centuries many similar episodes were recorded.

A reliable sighting took place in 1905, when two members of the Zoological Society of London saw a sea-serpent for themselves. Travelling aboard the *Valhalla* off the coast of Brazil, Meade Waldo and Michael Nicholl, were on deck when they first spotted what they believed to be a fin. As Waldo later wrote: '... I saw a large fin or frill sticking out of the water, dark seaweed-brown in colour and somewhat crinkled at the edge.

'It was apparently about 6 feet in length and projected from 18 inches to 2 feet from the water. I could see under the water to the rear of the frill, the shape of a considerable body. A great head and neck rose out of the water in front of the frill. The neck appeared to be about the thickness of a man's body. The head had a very turtle-like appearance, as had the eye.

'It moved its neck from side to side in a peculiar manner; the colour of its head and neck was dark brown above and whitish below.'

Within 14 hours, a second sighting was witnessed by the 1st and 3rd mate, who pointed it out to another of the ship's company. This time it did not properly break the surface but contented itself by

ABOVE: *Most sightings occur on warm, fine days. Could some unknown predator be following shoals of fish affected by the barometric pressure?*

LEFT: *A medieval artist's impresion of the 'kraken', a legendary sea monster which destroyed ships.*

swimming slightly faster than the ship (which was moving at 8.5 knots) and causing such a 'commotion in the water' that it 'looked as if a submarine was going along just below the surface.'

Writing in 1924, John Lockhart said in his *Mysteries of the Sea,* 'most of the witnesses [to the sea-serpent] agree on its outstanding features: it is a long serpentine creature: it has a series of humps; its head is rather like a horse's; its colour is dark on top and light below; it moves by undulations up and down; it appears during the summer months ... it is harmless, for it never actually attacks anybody.' Presumably the serpent had learnt better manners since the days of Aristotle!

In April 1977, the Japanese fishing vessel *Zuiyo-maru,* trawling off the coast of Christchurch, New Zealand, found a bizarre corpse in its nets. The carcase was about 33 feet (10 m) long, and it was estimated that it had been dead about a month. Although much of the skin had fallen away as it had decomposed, some of the tissue had turned to adipocere – a solid white soapy substance – which had preserved the red muscle tissue under it. No-one on board had ever seen anything like it, but because it stank to high heaven, they were unwilling to carry it all the way back to Japan for forensic tests. Instead, they threw it back into the water – but not before the captain took four photographs of the carcase, and drew several detailed sketches, noting accurately its dimensions.

News of this find was not given to the world's media until July 20th, when it caused a sensation. Perhaps it was nothing more than a basking shark, said one cautious lobby. Others suggested it may have been a giant sea-lion or a shell-less sea-turtle.

ABOVE: *The skeleton of a plesiosaur, extinct for 70 million years. Loch Ness is too cold for reptiles, but some experts believe dinosaurs were warm-blooded.*

In September of that year a symposium on the possible identity of the creature was held in Tokyo, and attended by experts in subjects as diverse (and specific) as immunology, mammology, comparative anatomy and marine paleontology. They studied the photographs, sketches, and some tiny shreds of tissue taken from the creature's fins, but came to no conclusion, except that they were *of no known species in the modern world.*

Some commentators remarked, however, that the monster had distinct affinities with the prehistoric plesiosaur, which supposedly died out around 70 million years ago. As very little of the seabed has been mapped, who is to say what bizarre creatures are still to be discovered?

The Hunt is On!

It is worth remembering that for years Western explorers of Africa regularly reported sightings of huge, hairy man like beasts of immense strength – only to be called liars or fools by the good folk at home. Then in 1903 one such creature was killed and its hide displayed in museums in Europe. Today, thanks largely to the dedicated zeal of Sir David Attenborough, the mountain gorilla is a familiar part of the natural world.

It is also worth noting that creatures once thought to be extinct have been found alive and well in our time. In 1938 fishermen caught a strange fish off the coast of South Africa. It turned out to be a coelacanth – a prehistoric fish dating back at least 350 million years – and one that had previously been deemed as dead as the dinosaurs.

However, even if we accept the possibility that a large unknown creature could lurk in the peaty waters of Loch Ness, what is the actual evidence for its existence?

Although there were several reported sightings of Nessie in the late 19th century, not until the 1930s was popular interest first awakened. It was in 1933 that several people reported that they had encountered the creature. Imaginations were really captured after the 'surgeon's picture' of the Monster was published in a London newspaper. In November 1933 Lt-Commander Rupert Gould began an energetic investigation of the sightings, talking to as many eyewitnesses around the loch as he could find.

Gould soon realised that the animal in question was, if it existed at all, unlikely to be easy to identify – for several reasons. For one thing, the species may date back to prehistoric times, and for another its sheer bulk would mean that most of its body would never be seen above water. Gould suggested that an airship might usefully be employed to find and identify the beast, but sadly, it never was.

In December 1933, the Daily Mail sponsored the first major attempt to find Nessie. A big game hunter, Marmaduke Weatherall, and a professional photographer, Gustav Pauli, were engaged at great expense. The two were to be seen on their launch the *Penguin* investigating around the shoreline. At last their patience was rewarded.

There, deep in the undergrowth by the loch, they found a large footprint, apparently made by a huge unknown creature. The excitement was immense – until the 'Nessie spoor' was revealed to have been made by a dried hippopotamus foot (otherwise in use as an umbrella stand).

However, after the Daily Mail sponsored hunt for Nessie, open season for hoaxers

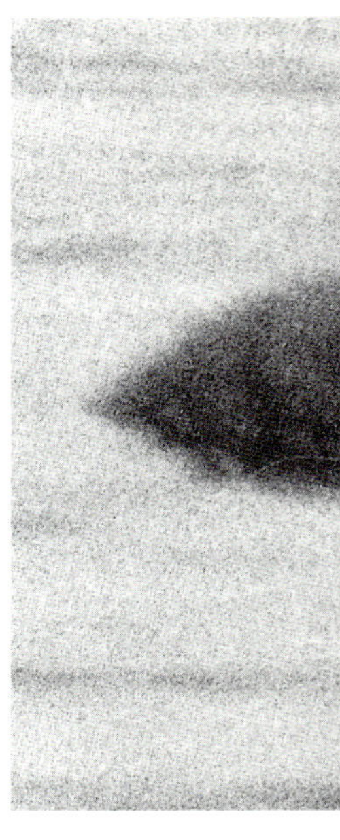

LEFT: *One of the classic 'Nessie' photographs: taken in 1974 it seems to show a partly submerged animal with a long neck and massive body.*

at Loch Ness was unofficially declared.

One Mr Robert Kenneth Wilson, was driving round Loch Ness, (close to Invermoriston) while on holiday in April 1934, when he saw something very unusual break the surface of the lake. Grabbing his camera, he took a total of four shots – two of which have survived, thus securing what was to become one of the most enduring, and controversial, images of the 20th century. The photographs showed a long arched neck protruding from the water, with the top part of a thick body just visible under the ripples. Had he really captured on camera the legendary Loch Ness Monster?

The road along which Mr Wilson drove had been improved in the previous year affording a clear view of the loch at that point – which may explain why there was such a spate of Nessie sightings after that time. Or perhaps the explosions needed to clear the site had disturbed the sleeping 'beastie'?

Whatever the explanation, the photograph was published in the Daily Mail, causing a great stir – and argument that rages to this day. On the one hand, sceptics say that the photograph shows nothing more than the tail of a diving otter seen out of scale, but on the other hand some argue that the general appearance of the creature is remarkably consistent with dozens of eyewitness descriptions.

In the following summer came Sir Edward Mountain's Loch Ness Expedition, its team consisting of 20 unemployed men from Inverness, who were stationed around the loch every day. Under the leadership of a Captain Fraser they did secure some interesting, and controversial photographs of something large in the water, but were rewarded with nothing conclusive. *continued on page 12*

FAR LEFT: *Considerable controversy surrounds this photograph made by Anthony Shiels in 1977. Over the years hoaxers have not helped genuine research in the loch.*

ABOVE: *The image which began 20th-century interest in the Monster: the famous 'surgeon's photograph' taken on April 19th 1934 by Harley Street consultant R. K. Wilson.*

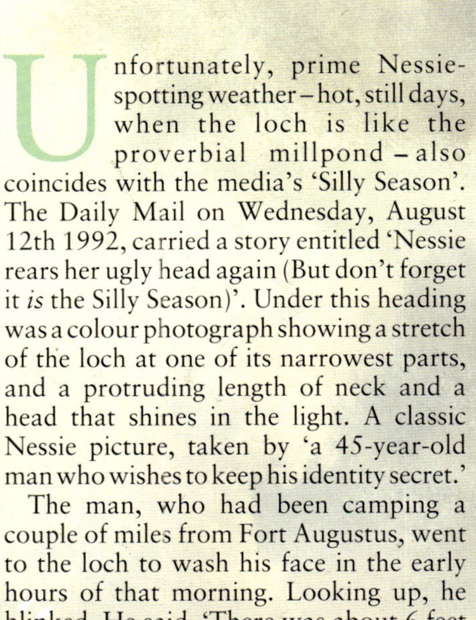

Unfortunately, prime Nessie-spotting weather – hot, still days, when the loch is like the proverbial millpond – also coincides with the media's 'Silly Season'. The Daily Mail on Wednesday, August 12th 1992, carried a story entitled 'Nessie rears her ugly head again (But don't forget it *is* the Silly Season)'. Under this heading was a colour photograph showing a stretch of the loch at one of its narrowest parts, and a protruding length of neck and a head that shines in the light. A classic Nessie picture, taken by 'a 45-year-old man who wishes to keep his identity secret.'

The man, who had been camping a couple of miles from Fort Augustus, went to the loch to wash his face in the early hours of that morning. Looking up, he blinked. He said, 'There was about 6 feet of a long neck and head and she was a blackish dark brown. She seemed to be looking right at me and I thought she was going to come to the shore. My camera (a Boots 110EF pocket model) was lying by the tree . . . and I made a dive for it.

'I scrambled back. She was about 40 yards out, still looking in my direction. I was trembling and my heart was pounding but I managed to knock off four shots.

'At one stage she opened her mouth. I thought she was going to make her breakfast of me.'

After submerging for five minutes, the beast resurfaced, together with four or five humps. The witness said, 'It was as if a miniature waterfall was cascading from the front hump'. Then she swam slowly away from him and submerged.

ILLUSTRATION: A *contemporary artist's reconstruction of the plesiosaur-like animal which naturalist Sir Peter Scott and many others believed the Loch Ness Monster to be.*

The negatives were examined at the RAF's photographic laboratory; Flight Lieutenant Caroline Smith said, 'We would say they have not been tampered with or touched up.' A Kodak scientist, Roger Flint, said after examining them, 'It is a genuine photograph of something, although we have no comment about the image.'

The newspaper, which carried the original 'surgeon's picture' in 1933, juggled its mixture of factual reporting and snide comment uneasily. Perhaps one reason for this sitting on the fence stemmed from recent discoveries of serious anomalies in the Wilson photograph, which at the very least cast doubt on its authenticity. Yet, tantalisingly, the surgeon's picture, real or false, matches some eyewitness descriptions of the beast.

Occasional sightings continued to be made during the rest of the 1930s. Nessie was quiet during the war years: popular newspapers and the public imagination were preoccupied with the less attractive monsters born of Nazism. But the activities of the war ministry (and later the ministry of defence) in Loch Ness may – if the records are ever made public – add a fascinating missing chapter to the Loch Ness Monster story.

In 1951 Lachlan Stuart, a local man, saw something that he thought was a powerboat. Then when it appeared to show three distinct humps above the water, all moving together at great speed, he grabbed his box camera and took some photographs. He captured the humps, but not the head, which he saw dipping and rising several times, and which he described as looking 'like a sheep's'. Sceptics say that the humps could have been three separate objects – rocks, perhaps. However Lachlan Stuart, confessed to a local resident Richard Frere that the three monster humps were in fact, covered straw bales!

Of all the dozens of other photographs that are allegedly of the monster, some have become classics, often for the wrong reasons. For example Mr P A McNab's 1955 picture of large humps just off Castle Urquart may just be 'doctored', and the so-called 'Loch Ness muppet' – a tree-trunk like neck of the monster with open mouth, taken by Anthony 'Doc' Shiels in 1977 – has since been questioned even by those inclined to believe in the existence of Nessie.

The best known film evidence for the creature is a cine film of something large, and apparently animate, moving at speed through the water. Taken in 1960 by

ABOVE TOP: *The 'spray photograph' apparently showing something animate breaking the surface; it was taken by Hugh Gray on November 12th 1933.*

ABOVE: *One of the many 'hump photographs' which some believe to be misidentified boat wakes, wind slicks, waterbirds and even swimming deer.*

monster-hunter extraordinary, the late Tim Dinsdale, this remains controversial.

It was shot from the mouth of the River Foyers, which runs into Loch Ness from the south. It shows a hump, at first moving slowly away from him, then picking up speed as it begins to submerge. Dinsdale submitted the film for analysis to the Joint Air Reconnaissance Intelligence Centre (JARIC), and their opinion was that it showed an object that was approximately $5\frac{1}{2}$ feet (1.7m) wide, moving at a speed of about 10mph (16 kph) and was 'probably animate'. It was not a boat, despite the inevitable claims of the sceptics.

Tim Dinsdale was a prime mover in the establishment of the Loch Ness Investigation Bureau, the Loch Morar Project and the research of Dr Rines, besides being a close friend of Sir Peter Scott. His personal belief in Nessie was complete – after all, he had seen her.

Tim Dinsdale was noted for his interest in the paranormal. His archival studies of the world's legendary lake monsters and sea serpents enabled him to place Nessie in a wider context. He firmly believed that the beast was a throwback to prehistoric times, one of the serpent-like creatures that appear again and again in mythology, very probably something like a plesiosaur. One of his pieces of cinematic research seemed to reveal that the monster, although never known to have attacked a man in modern times, may accidentally have caused a famous death.

Intrigued by a simple stone cairn by the lochside erected by the local people 'to a very gallant Gentleman', he discovered that it commemorates John Cobb's fatal attempt on the world water-speed record on September 29th 1952. Cobb's motorboat *Crusader* disintegrated when it struck 'an area of disturbed water' in the centre of the loch.

Witnesses said that Cobb realised he was about to hit several large ripples that rose abruptly from the surface of the water and closed his throttle. But it was too late; the boat bounced up and down two or three times and then disintegrated, throwing him to his instant death.

Dinsdale analysed newsreel film and contemporary reports of the event, and became convinced that Cobb's powerful boat had disturbed the beast beneath. Perhaps its hurried efforts to escape caused huge V-shaped ripples to cut across the boat's path, making it buck violently before smashing to pieces.

ABOVE: *Tim Dinsdale.*
BELOW: *John Cobb.*

ABOVE: *It has been suggested that John Cobb's tragic accident in 1952 was caused by sudden unexplained ripples.*

During his years of involvement with the Loch Ness investigations, Tim Dinsdale discovered several fascinating facts about the subject: some more off-beat than others. He came to believe in a jinx that pervaded attempts to find conclusive evidence of the

Monster. It was a history of near-misses with suddenly recalcitrant equipment – something that most subsequent investigators were to discover to their cost. In his 1976 book *The Leviathans*, Dinsdale writes, 'On two occasions camera crews had near-misses, when for one reason or another they moved station only to find that the move had cost them a dramatic piece of film. Some of the older local people attributed this to supernatural influence: shades of the dreaded Loch Ness 'hoodoo', known by some of the Americans (researchers) simply as 'the Hex'. A number of the people at LNI (Loch Ness Investigation Bureau) secretly believed in it, because they found the continuing near-misses impossible to explain away on the basis of chance. . .'

Another bizarre phenomenon – possibly psychological in origin – connected with the Monster was also touched upon in *The Leviathans*. Dinsdale noted that fellow researcher Ted Holliday had written to him: 'Had a curious impression when questioning (witnesses) . . . I couldn't put it in my report. When people are confronted by this fantastic animal at close quarters they seem to be stunned. There is something strange about Nessie that has nothing to do with size or appearance. . . .'

Dinsdale, who had come across the same thing in his own interviews of witnesses adds, 'Perhaps the explanation lies in the sense of unreality, dreaming, almost, which affects one when looking at the beast. It is as though one is looking at a unicorn. Something impossible, absurd, incredible, the blatant flesh-and-blood existence of which has quite a bemusing effect.'

A more mundane discovery made by the great monster hunter was that sightings of Nessie at the surface of the loch tended to happen on fine days, when there was hardly a ripple on the water. Dinsdale came to know that Nessie-spotting was a waste of time in days of wind and rain.

One possible explanation for Nessie favouring good weather, unless it merely shares the universal preference for blue skies, is that it is in keeping with the behaviour of bottom-dwelling fish, such

ABOVE: *One of the underwater photographs taken by the Academy of Applied Science, Boston.*

as loaches or catfish, which surface in warm weather due to barometric pressure. There are certainly enough accounts of her tendency to do so.

Returning to the film evidence for Nessie, perhaps the most famous footage after Tim Dinsdale's is that shot by Richard Reynor during the Loch Ness Expedition of 1967. It is exceptional for its technical quality. Taken from the north end of the loch, the film shows a wake, at the head of which a solid object appears – ducking back under the water as a boat appears in the frame. Although the object was certainly animate, Raynor was willing to concede that it may have been waterbirds or an otter, but JARIC estimated that the part that broke the surface alone was 7 feet (2m) long – a little on the large size for an otter!

Hoaxers may gloat and sceptics sneer, but there are now over 1000 documented sightings of the Monster. Eyewitness accounts may be less compelling than photographs or film, but it cannot be ignored. Undoubtedly some sightings were the product of wishful thinking, misidentification of natural objects or phenomena, or perhaps of the effects of one 'wee dram' too many. But for the most part, the accounts are those of sober, honest people who do not seek publicity, but simply want to tell their amazing tale.

Researchers concluded that the sheer weight of sightings indicated there was a case deserving further investigation. The first chronicler of the Loch Ness sightings was Lt-Commander Gould, who, in his 1934 book The *Loch Ness Monster*, described 42 sightings from the period May 1923-May 1933. After him came Mrs Constance Whyte (one of the founders of the Loch Ness Investigation Bureau), whose 1957 book *More Than A Legend* listed over 60 eyewitness accounts. Since then there have been hundreds more, most of them sharing remarkably consistent details – in itself either a testament to the background reading of the hoaxers or the authenticity of the story!

ABOVE: *Two stills from a video shot by wildlife photographer Erik Beckjord in 1983. The white area (top right) shows something unexplained breaking the surface.*

Here are some of the accounts:

In August 1960 Mr Lowrie made a sighting from the deck of his yacht *Finola*. Lowrie wrote in the boat's log: 'All hands on deck witness a curious form coming up astern between 6 and 10 knots looking like a couple of ducks, occasionally submerging, and a neck-like protrusion breaking surface. The Monster – nothing less. As it came abeam we were fascinated, so much that it had passed to starboard before anyone remembered we had an old camera on board . . . After ten minutes it swung away to starboard towards Aldourie Point and some photographs were taken. It swam quickly causing considerable disturbance and showing a large area of green and brown . . . (we) agreed we would say nothing and take care of photographs . . . LOG NOTES: (It) made bow wave similar to Finola's and appeared frightened by noise . . . certainly appeared to follow *Finola* for a time'.

Father Gregory's Sighting

Unfortunately, due perhaps to the 'jinx' or just to a state bordering on shock, Mr Lowrie's photographs were indistinct.

Monster hunter Ted Holiday interviewed a 'Mr McI' in 1963 almost immediately after he heard of the man's close encounter with the beast. Mr McI was adamant about Nessie's appearance. 'The Monster's neck came out of the water quickly. It was powerful and of considerable thickness – a column of at least 1 foot in diameter. The head was held at a slight angle to the neck. . . it reminded me of a bulldog, that is, flat on top with a powerful lower face. I could see no eyes or tentacles. Colour of the head was blackish brown. The head was wide and extremely ugly. Part of a hump was also visible . . . the beast was hairy. . . the neck was fringed by what looked like coarse black hair . . . it reminded me of the mane seen on Highland cattle.'

Summing up, Mr McI said, 'there is certainly a weird beastie in the loch . . . but I don't expect anyone to believe in the Monster until they have seen it with their own eyes.'

Many of the witnesses whose accounts are given in Tim Dinsdale's *The Leviathans* comment on Nessie's ability to sink down into the water, as if being pulled from underneath. Its neck is commonly described as looking like a 'telegraph pole' and the suddenness of its appearance is usually heralded by 'a great commotion' or 'huge turbulence' in the water. And sometimes there appear to be more than one animal swimming together; after all, if Nessie is real, she would need to be one of a family!

In 1970 Tim Dinsdale and his colleagues aboard the research craft *Water Horse* in Urquhart Bay had seen a 'telegraph pole-like object moving through the water, protruding at least 10 feet above the surface.' They felt that people might think this estimate of Nessie's neck to be an exaggeration – until along came the perfect corroboration of their story.

On October 19th 1971, Father Gregory Brusey of the Benedictine Abbey in Fort Augustus and a friend, Roger Pugh, saw 'a terrific commotion in the waters of the bay . . . in the mindst . . . we saw quite distinctly the neck of the beast standing out of the water to . . . a height of about 10 feet. It swam towards us at a slight angle, and after about 20 seconds slowly disappeared, the neck immersing at a slight angle. We were at a distance of about 300 yards . . .' Father Gregory's eyewitness account remains one of the most compelling pieces of evidence for the existence of the Loch Ness Monster.

ABOVE: *The Benedictine Abbey in Fort Augustus.*

BELOW LEFT: *Tim Dinsdale.*

Although members of the public continued to see the creature, the first scientific investigation was organised in 1962, when the Loch Ness Investigation Bureau was set up by David James MP, Constance Whyte, Richard Fitter, and the naturalist Peter Scott. Their aim was to gather information and to promote research, and they soon set up a professional surveillance programme.

In 1968 the Bureau enlisted the aid of American sponsors and technicians, mounting the first serious underwater investigation of the loch. They used sophisticated sonar equipment instead of photography – modern technology to seek what they believed might be a living prehistoric relic.

BELOW: *'Operation Deepscan' whose sonar curtain made deep contacts which scientists cannot explain.*

Sonar is essentially the underwater equivalent of radar, transmitting sound instead of radio waves into the water. These sound waves 'bounce' off any object of a different density to the surrounding water; the greater the difference, the greater the echo that will bounce back. It echoes off both solid objects and volumes of air, which enables it to detect fish or aquatic animals by echoing off their swim bladders or lungs.

Two main sonar devices used in Loch Ness were the echo sounder and scanning sonar. The echo sounder was used mostly for sounding the varying depths of the loch; it operates by emitting a sonar pulse and records the time lapse between sending it out and receiving the sonar echo from the floor of the loch. A mathematical conversion then gives the depth at that point.

Scanning sonar – frequently used by fishermen for locating shoals of fish – has a sonar 'beam' that can be swung towards possible targets. At Loch Ness the sonar devices are usually mounted on expedition boats on the loch, or on fixed stations on the shore line.

As early as 1962 a combined Oxford and Cambridge team secured tantalisingly strong echo sounder traces – much stronger than those produced by say, large active salmon. Three boats equipped with 28-kiloHertz echo sounders moved together along the loch, attempting either to locate the beast or to drive it to the end of the loch. This failed, but the team hastened to point out the disadvantages of the system they used – for example, it was not possible to get echoes from the bottom. However, they did manage to get some large 'contacts' later, although once again, their evidence was not conclusive.

In 1968 a team from Birmingham University, working with the Loch Ness Investigation Bureau, brought a much more powerful sonar scanner to the loch. Set up on a fixed station at Urquart Bay, it monitored the waters continuously for 150 hours. On August 28th it tracked a large object rising from the floor of the loch at a speed of 7.5 mph (12 kph), and they also tracked another that travelled at 17 mph (25 kph), speeds that indicated that the objects were animate, yet unlikely to be shoals of fish.

Science Joins the Search

In 1969 the Vickers Oceanics' submersible *Pisces* made contact with a large object about 50 feet (16 m) off the bottom which then disappeared hastily when the craft drew near.

Also in that year a small private submarine the *Viperfish*, built by American Dan Taylor, came to the loch with the intention of firing darts at the contacts to try to get a tissue sample. Obviously this would aid enormously in identifying the elusive creature, but Taylor, like many another before and since, was defeated by the poor visibility of the peaty waters.

Around this time, more bizarre attempts to lure the Monster to the surface were attempted, some using foul-smelling bait made of snake hormone and other 'witches' brew' ingredients. But Nessie remained aloof.

In 1974 it was decided to investigate Loch Ness and Loch Morar (which has a similar monster tradition) in tandem. The one great advantage of Loch Morar is that the water is very clear – ideal for surveying the depths in a manned submersible.

Machan, a small underwater observation vehicle, was manned by a team of researchers and aided by the use of underwater television. Their brief was not merely to locate a 'monster', but to identify it, and to find the remains of its dead relatives. Unfortunately, the results were negative.

There was, for a time, a serious move to bring in teams of trained dolphins to join the researchers, but the obstacles proved overwhelming: dolphins cannot adapt to freshwater; there were enormous logistical problems involved in transporting and feeding them; and they are basically too intelligent to agree to take part in anything that is uncomfortable (or, sceptics might add, anything that is obviously a wild goose chase).

In 1972, underwater photography made the first contribution to the controversial evidence in the hunt for Nessie. Of course the peaty water hampered both the maintenance of such equipment and the identification of anything unusual picked up by it, so the new computer-enhancement techniques proved extremely useful.

In that year, Dr Robert Rines of the Academy of Applied Science, Boston, USA, brought the latest monitoring and photographic equipment to Loch Ness. Almost immediately he succeeded in capturing the 'flipper' picture with a time-lapse camera fitted with a strobe flash. This, by now famous, photograph, seems to show a large diamond-shaped flipper or fin close to the camera. Naturally it has provoked a storm of controversy, which shows no sign of dying down. Also there is some evidence that the published versions may have been retouched. But if it is indeed the flipper of a large animal, it belongs to a creature unknown to science.

Later pictures taken by the Rines team appear to show a close-up of a monstrous horned head, its symmetry suggesting that it belongs to a living creature. The pictures once described as 'bagpipes in a snowstorm' were claimed to show a reddish-brown beast about 12 feet (4 m) long with an arching neck of about 8 feet (2.5 m) long which tallied remarkably well with the majority of eyewitness descriptions.

Unfortunately, experts have dismissed two-thirds of the pictures in this sequence as being of definitely inanimate objects, and sceptics claim to have debunked the

In 1969 Dan Taylor (ABOVE) *attempted to obtain tissue samples with his submarine* Viperfish. *The 'fin picture'* (BELOW) *and*

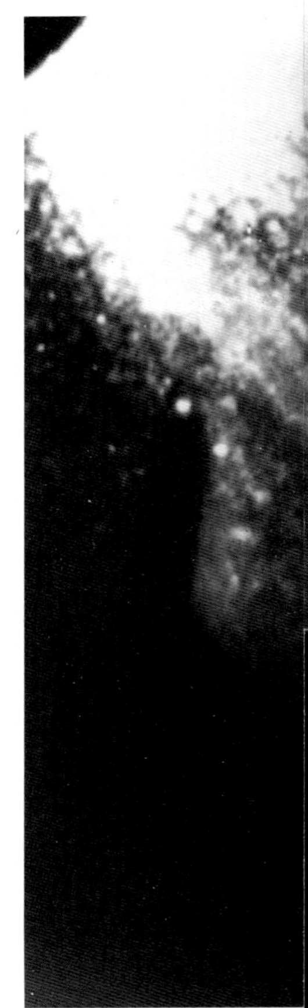

'gargoyle head' photograph (TOP RIGHT) *were taken by Dr Robert Rines* (RIGHT).

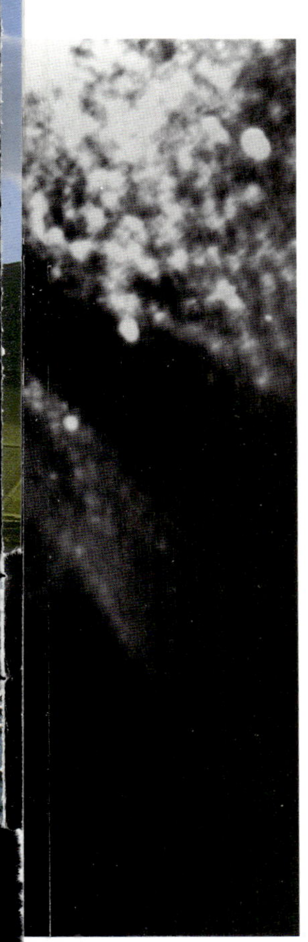

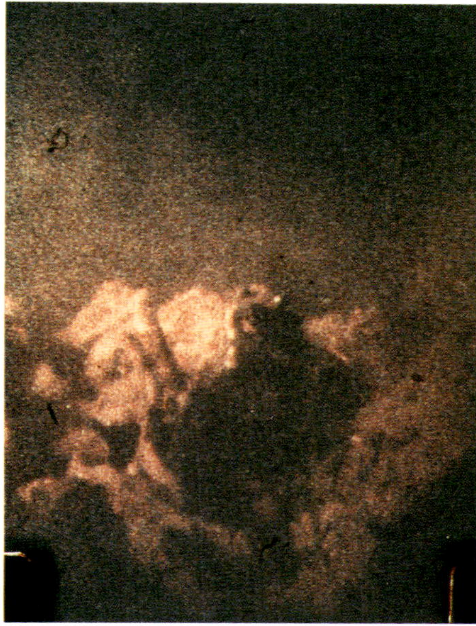

'head' as being a curiously-formed waterlogged sunken treestump. These pictures, however, still have the ability to cause shivers to creep up and down the spine.

The underwater pictures, together with a huge amount of other evidence for the existence of Nessie, were presented to members of both Houses of Parliament and members of the Press on December 10th 1975. It was received relatively politely but the feeling afterwards was that it converted no one, believers and sceptics remaining poles apart.

Interestingly, however, some of the world's top research scientists were more positive, about Dr Rines' underwater pictures. For example, G R Zug, Ph.D., Curator of the Division of Reptiles and Amphibians at the Smithsonian Institute, wrote: 'I believe that these data indicate the presence of large animals in Loch Ness, but are insufficient to identify them.' And in answer to many standard sceptical 'explanations', Alan Gillespie of the Jet Propulsion Laboratory, California Institute of Technology, said 'I see no evidence that they are pictures of a model, toy... or whatever. I emphasise, I detect no evidence of fraud. These objects are not patterns of algae, sediment or gas bubbles.'

Closer to home, naturalist Sir Peter Scott (then Chairman of the World Wildlife Fund), waxed enthusiastic, 'In conjunction with a number of earlier records, on film and in still photographs which cannot be explained in terms of known phenomena, the underwater pictures leave no further doubt in my mind that large animals exist in Loch Ness.'

To back up his belief in the existence of Nessie, Sir Peter invented a formal scientific name for it – *Nessiteras Rhombopteryx*, or 'Ness wonder with a diamond fin'. Unfortunately, anagram experts discovered that by juggling the letters around you can get 'monster hoax by Sir Peter S'! The odds against this happening by pure chance are astronomical. Inevitably there were charges against Sir Peter and his pro-Nessie colleagues of a deliberate hoax, along the lines of the infamous 'Piltdown Man' episode where fossil remains of an early hominid – the so-called 'missing link' – were deliberately fabricated. Later, Dr Rines got his own back with some more letter juggling, this time coming up with 'Yes, both pix are Monsters. R'!

What if Nessie is Found?

Since the heady days of presenting evidence to Westminster, Nessie hunters have continued to use the most up-to-date equipment to try to find her.

Underwater strobe cameras have been replaced by underwater television but sonar remains the basis of ongoing research. However, nothing beats sheer manpower, or so it seemed in 1987, when 'Operation Deepscan' went into action. The most ambitious attempt ever to detect the monster, it involved a flotilla of 24 motor launches, each equipped with sonar, spending a week patrolling the loch in unison. All this effort was rewarded by three strong contacts. One of these – a sonar echo from a 'large and moving' object 200 feet (67 m) down – remains unexplained.

Tantalising and fascinating, the beast of Loch Ness continues to exert its magnetism across the world, as the 1990 'Monster Hunt Weekend' revealed. A not-too-serious media event, it provided the focus for an astonishing number of foreign television crews, some Japanese teams even setting up their own satellite transmitters on the banks of the loch. Even this jokey weekend provided some evidence. During filming aboard the boat chartered by the Oceanscan team, the crew became excited by an unexplained 'blip' on their sonar screen. Witnessed by a four-strong team from the ITV children's programme *Motormouth* and a Japanese film crew, it seemed to show a large, animate object moving at speed at the bottom of the loch. Unfortunately, the underwater camera was pointing in the wrong direction at the time, a hazard that Oceanscan's team acknowledged wearily to be all too common.

The latest research project centred on Nessie is Project Urquhart, founded by a British businessman and BBC newscaster Nick Witchell (who once spent five months in a shack by the loch waiting, unsuccessfully, to see the Monster). Using the very latest technology, the project aims to investigate the loch's flora and fauna, some of which may have escaped the attentions of scientists, due to the sheer depth of water involved. And if a certain familiar creature should offer itself for examination by the researchers of Project Urquhart, so much the better.

RIGHT: *Perseus had good reason to slay the dragon, but many innocent creatures have suffered through Man's ignorance and fear.*